# BEFORE THE TSUNAMI

*A common-sense guide to avoid damages before, during, and after divorce*

**Dr. Roger Avila**

# Copyright 2025 Dr. Roger Avila All Rights Reserved

This book is subject to the condition that no part of this book is to be reproduced, transmitted in any form or means, electronic or mechanical, stored in a retrieval system, photocopied, recorded, canned, or otherwise. Any of these actions require the proper written permission of the author.

Published by **Book Writing Craft**

4900 California Avenue, Tower B, 2nd Floor, Bakersfield, CA 93309

**877-286-0704**

# AUTHOR'S BIOGRAPHY

I was born in Cuba, in the small town of Holguín, located about 12 hours east of Havana. I moved to Canada in 2000 with the intention of attending the University of Toronto. However, admission is quite competitive; out of 1,000 applicants, only 25 are accepted. To prepare, I first studied English at an ESL school for a few months. While I needed to earn a living, I was never keen on government programs designed to assist immigrants. From 2000 to 2006, I worked a variety of jobs. My first job involved selling candy apples near the beaches, after which I became a busboy and then a waiter at the same restaurant. I later joined a marketing company that collaborated with clients like the Shopping Channel to help them sell their products. Eventually, I secured a position as a dental assistant. In my spare time, I sold RRSPs and eventually enrolled at the University of Toronto to study dentistry. After graduating, I returned to the same office where I had worked as an assistant. A year later, I opened my first dental practice, and today I own three offices.

In my free time, I enjoy collecting coins, dancing salsa, trading cryptocurrency, spending time with my sons and my wonderful girlfriend, traveling, and making the most of life. Now, at 51 years old, I reflect on my journey and acknowledge that despite going through a divorce—which I consider my biggest failure—life has taught me resilience and the importance of moving forward. One phrase I often use is "It is what it is," but another that resonates with me is "Let's make it happen."

DR. ROGER AVILA

*To my amazing two sons, Rogy and Georgy.*
*This book is a small project where I wanted to leave my thoughts in a written format for you two to be prepared for the worst but be ready to have a beautiful family like the one I lost.*
*I never thought I would get divorced,*
*I am sorry I put you through all those harsh times.*
*I hope you never go through it, and if you do you*
*get out of it in an honorable way.*

# PROLOGUE

Divorce is one of those things you never really plan for, yet when it happens, it changes everything. It's not just the end of a marriage—it's the unraveling of a life you once knew, the breaking apart of dreams you built together. It's painful, messy, and sometimes, it feels impossible to get through.

When I sat down to write this book, I wanted to understand divorce in a way that went beyond the legal process or the clichés. I wanted to hear from real people—those who have lived it, fought through it, and somehow found a way forward. Every story in these pages is a piece of that journey, a raw and honest look at what it means to lose love and rebuild in its absence.

I've spoken to so many who have been through the storm—some still caught in its chaos, others who have come out the other side stronger than they ever thought possible. Their experiences are all different, but the emotions are strikingly similar: grief, anger, uncertainty, and, eventually, the quiet resilience that allows them to start over.

You'll find pain in these stories, but you'll also find hope. Because as devastating as divorce can be, it doesn't have to be the end. It can be a new beginning, even if it doesn't feel that way at first. My hope is that these voices remind you that you're not alone—that healing is possible, and that even in the hardest moments, there's a way forward.

# INTRODUCTION

Divorce is one of life's most challenging transitions. It leaves behind feelings, emotions, financial accomplishments, properties, dreams, memories, promises, and kids. As a result, one of the partners will become a slave to the other following financial abuse enforced by the law, causing a massive unfair enrichment and separations of assets, in which many end up being mentally, emotionally, and physically abused to the point that many decide to end their lives. In the process, individuals, corporations, institutions, and governments massively benefit financially from the separation of what one day was a beautiful union.

This book is written with the intention of enlightening those who are blinded by love and lust.

This book also serves as a guide to friends, family members, and even co-workers, supporting those embarking on one of life's most beautiful journeys—marriage—that can also, at times, become one of the most destructive paths; hence the title of the book.

Cities, like relationships, are built on strong pillars like trust, understanding, and compromise; without strong foundations, none will survive a devastating phenomenon like a Tsunami (divorce).

You will find that every time you present this guide to someone, they already have an answer for you—answers such as:

- That would never happen to me.
- She/he is not like that.
- I am getting married for life.

- Our love is impossible to break.

All these answers show how blind and naive people can be when making important decisions of their lives. They know the venue, the guest list, the size of the ring, and even where they're going for the honeymoon. But they haven't talked about the important stuff, like how many kids they want, what kind of pets they'll have, or whether they're living in a house or an apartment.

# TABLE OF CONTENTS

Author's Biography

Prologue

Introduction

*Chapter 1* Understanding Divorce

*Chapter 2* Things to Consider and Discuss Before Getting Married

*Chapter 3* Preparing for Divorce

*Chapter 4* Experiencing Divorce

*Chapter 5* Dealing with the Aftermath of Divorce

*Chapter 6* Everyone Benefits from a Divorce

*Chapter 7* *Harmful Effects of Divorce*

*Chapter 8* Potential Financial Implications for a Wealthy Individual

*Chapter 9* Marriage

*Chapter 10* How Divorce can Harm you Financially

*Chapter 11* Cohabitation Agreement

Funny Phrases, Serious Reflections

Final Thoughts

Percentage of Births Out of Wedlock (1964 vs. 2014)

Percent of US Births Outside of Wedlock by Major Group (1964-2014)

Percent of Children Living with Two Cohabiting Parents vs. Sole Parent (2014)

# CHAPTER 1

## Understanding Divorce

"Heartbreak is a loss. Divorce is a piece of paper."

—Taylor Jenkins Reid

Divorce is a significant and often life-changing event that brings a mix of emotions, challenges, and transformations. Understanding what divorce entails can help you navigate this journey with clarity and resilience.

# THE EMOTIONAL LANDSCAPE

Divorce is not just the end of a marriage; it's the end of a shared vision of the future. This can lead to feelings of sadness, anger, guilt, relief, or even fear of the unknown. Each person experiences divorce differently, and it's okay to feel a mix of emotions that might seem contradictory. For instance, you might feel liberated and heartbroken at the same time. Recognizing and validating these emotions is an essential step toward healing.

It's important to remember that the emotional toll of divorce doesn't just affect the couple involved; children, family members, and friends often feel its ripple effects. Open communication and emotional support can make this transition smoother for everyone.

# MYTHS AND MISCONCEPTIONS

Many misconceptions surround divorce, which can create unnecessary pressure or guilt. Here are a few common myths:

1. Divorce is always a failure: False. Many view divorce as a sign of failure, but it can be a necessary step for personal growth and happiness.
2. Children are better off in an unhappy marriage: False. Staying in a toxic relationship can negatively impact children. Healthy co-parenting or separate households can provide a better environment.
3. Divorce is always a contentious process: False. While some divorces are contentious, many couples manage to part amicably, especially when they prioritize communication and cooperation.
4. Men always get the better deal: False. Divorce outcomes depend on various factors, including income, custody, and individual circumstances, rather than gender.
5. Divorce is quick and easy: False. The process can be lengthy and complicated, involving legal, emotional, and financial challenges.
6. You should wait until your children are grown to divorce: False. Timing varies for each family. Sometimes, making a change sooner can be more beneficial for all involved.
7. Divorce means you'll be alone forever: False. Many people

find love again after divorce. It can be an opportunity for personal growth and new relationships.

8. Infidelity is the main reason for divorce: False. While infidelity is a factor for some, many couples divorce due to communication issues, financial problems, or growing apart. Understanding these myths can help individuals navigate the complexities of divorce more effectively.

9. Divorce is a selfish decision. False

10. Divorce always results in long battles in court. False

11. Divorce could be a very emotional process. True

12. Should be avoided when children are involved. False

13. Spousal support is always guaranteed. False

14. Divorce is always financially devastating. False

15. Divorce is always time-consuming. False

16. Divorce always leads to court battles. False

17. In case your spouse cheats court will always take your side. False

18. Courts favor moms in court cases. False

19. It's a quick process. False

20. You need grounds to file for a divorce. False

21. Marital assets are always split 50/50. False

# AN IDEAL RELATIONSHIP

An ideal relationship typically embodies several key qualities:

1. Communication: Open and honest dialogue is essential. Partners should feel comfortable discussing their thoughts, feelings, and concerns without fear of judgment.

2. Trust: A strong foundation of trust allows both partners to feel secure and confident in each other. This includes being reliable and keeping commitments.

3. Respect: Each partner values the other's opinions, boundaries, and individuality. This mutual respect fosters a healthy dynamic.

4. Support: Partners should be each other's biggest supporters, encouraging growth and celebrating successes, while also providing comfort during tough times.

5. Shared Values and Goals: While differences can be enriching, having core values and long-term goals aligned can enhance compatibility and strengthen the bond.

6. Quality Time: Spending meaningful time together helps deepen the connection. This can include shared activities or simply enjoying each other's company.

7. Independence: While being together is important, maintaining individual identities and interests allows both partners to grow personally and contribute to the relationship.

8. Conflict Resolution: Disagreements are natural. An ideal relationship involves healthy conflict resolution strategies, where both partners can express their views and find compromises.

9. Affection and Intimacy: Physical and emotional intimacy plays a key role in maintaining closeness and connection, reinforcing the bond between partners.

10. Fun and Laughter: A sense of humor and the ability to have fun together can strengthen the relationship, making it more enjoyable and resilient in tough times.

An ideal relationship is not about perfection but rather about mutual growth, understanding, and a deep emotional connection.

# WHY DIVORCE HAPPENS

Every relationship is unique, and so are the reasons for its breakdown. Some of the most common causes of divorce include:

- **Lack of communication**: Misunderstandings, unresolved conflicts, or emotional distance can erode the foundation of a marriage.
- **Infidelity**: Trust is vital in any relationship, and infidelity often breaks that trust.
- **Financial stress**: Differences in financial habits, debts, or economic hardships can strain a marriage.
- **Growing apart**: Over time, couples may realize they have different goals, values, or interests.
- **Abuse**: Physical, emotional, or psychological abuse is a serious and valid reason to end a marriage.

Understanding why your marriage is ending can help you process your emotions and move forward with clarity. Remember, it's not about assigning blame but about acknowledging what didn't work and how to create a better future.

# MISTAKES A WIFE CAN MAKE THAT MAY HARM HER MARRIAGE[1]

There are fifteen mistakes a wife might unknowingly make that could put her marriage at risk. Take a moment to reflect on them and steer clear.

1. **CHALLENGING HER HUSBAND TO HIT HER**
   Blocking the doorway and daring your husband to raise his hand against you is a dangerous game. Many women have made this mistake and deeply regretted it. It's unwise and unnecessary.

2. **DARING HER HUSBAND TO SLEEP WITH ANOTHER WOMAN**
   Telling your husband to go ahead and sleep with another woman might seem like a way to prove a point, but it could backfire in ways you never imagined. Be careful what you challenge him to do—you may live to regret it.

3. **NEGLECTING HER APPEARANCE AFTER MARRIAGE**
   "I'm married now, who do I need to impress?" That was Mrs. Ade's response when someone asked why she dressed so poorly. Many married women make this mistake, thinking their looks no longer matter. But

neglecting oneself can have unintended consequences.

4. **DENYING HER HUSBAND SEX REGULARLY**
   A busy career is no excuse to deprive your husband of affection and intimacy. If he feels neglected, there are plenty of other women—secretaries, colleagues, even acquaintances at places of worship—who might be all too willing to offer him the attention he craves. Don't let frustration build to a breaking point.

5. **TRUSTING A FRIEND TO CARE FOR HER HUSBAND IN HER ABSENCE**
   "Please keep an eye on my husband while I'm away for a week," said Mrs. Rosa to her trusted friend. By the time she returned, that same friend had not only slept with her husband but later ran away with him. Be careful who you trust with your home and marriage.

6. **LEAVING HER HUSBAND IN THE CARE OF HER HOUSEMAID**
   When the maid handles everything—cooking, cleaning, childcare—you risk becoming disconnected from your own household. Some women unknowingly make it easy for someone else to step into their role.

7. **HIRING AN ATTRACTIVE, FULLY GROWN WOMAN AS A MAID**
   She's well-endowed, stylish, and carries herself like a model—yet she's your maid? This decision may lead to problems down the road.

8. **CHOOSING A MAID MORE ATTRACTIVE THAN HERSELF**
   Many women unknowingly bring competition into their home by hiring someone who could easily become their rival. Choose wisely when bringing a stranger into your household.

9. **FAILING TO GROW ALONGSIDE HER HUSBAND**
   Your husband is advancing in life—keeping up with

trends, engaging in business talks, and staying active on social media. Meanwhile, you're stuck in the past, uninterested in his world. If you don't grow together, you risk growing apart.

10. **NEGLECTING PRAYER AND SPIRITUAL SUPPORT FOR HER FAMILY**
A home that lacks spiritual guidance is more vulnerable to struggles. A wife who doesn't commit her family to God in prayer may find herself facing unnecessary challenges.

11. **CONSTANTLY CLASHING WITH HER MOTHER-IN-LAW**
Fighting your mother-in-law is a battle you are unlikely to win. She was your husband's first love in life—his protector and guide before you ever came into the picture. Choose peace over unnecessary conflict.

12. **DISCUSSING HER SEX LIFE WITH FRIENDS**
Sharing details about your intimate life might seem harmless, but it can backfire. A friend who learns too much might start comparing, observing, and eventually making a move on your husband. Guard your privacy.

13. **REPORTING HER HUSBAND TO HIS MOTHER**
Running to your mother-in-law with complaints about her son might seem like a good idea, but mothers naturally side with their children. Seeking advice is fine, but choose the right confidant.

14. **LETTING HER CHILDREN REPLACE HER HUSBAND**
Some women become so consumed with motherhood that their husbands feel sidelined. Placing the baby between you and your husband every night may seem practical, but over time, it can create distance.

15. **USING INTIMACY AS A WEAPON**
Sex should be a source of love and connection, not

a tool for manipulation. Some women use it to bargain or control their husbands, while others act uninterested, making their partners feel rejected. This kind of approach can slowly damage a marriage.

May we never be the architects of our own marital struggles. May God protect our homes and guide us to nurture love, respect, and harmony in our marriages. Amen.

# DECAPITATE MEDUSA (GET READY FOR BATTLE)

The expression "decapitate Medusa" refers to the mythological story of Perseus and Medusa from Greek mythology. Medusa is known for her hair of snakes and the ability to turn anyone who gazes at her into stone. Perseus, tasked with slaying her, uses a reflective shield to avoid her deadly gaze and ultimately decapitates her. In a broader context, the phrase can symbolize overcoming a formidable challenge or defeating a seemingly insurmountable adversary. It often represents the idea of confronting fears or obstacles directly and finding a way to triumph over them. Additionally, it may allude to the concept of eliminating a source of danger or threat, much like how Perseus removed the threat posed by Medusa.

The modern Medusas won't turn you into stone, but they could be very harmful in multiple ways.

Modern Medusas could:

1. Empty your bank accounts without telling you.

2. Take your kids away.

3. Talk bad behind your back and turn kids, family and friends against you.

4. Make you their slave using the law for you to pay them alimony.

5. Ask for a huge amount of child support.

6. Play with your brain and make you mentally ill.

7. Call the police on you for no reason.

8. Add you to a no-flight list by telling a judge how dangerous you are.

9. Ask for a restraining order based on lies.

10. Make you lose your job.

11. Slandering and creating lies about you and your capabilities.

It's important to approach sensitive topics like divorce and custody with care and empathy. While some individuals may engage in negative behaviors during or after a divorce, it's crucial to recognize that every situation is unique. Here are some general actions that could occur in contentious divorces, but these are not universally applicable:

1. Restricting Communication: Some may limit or control communication between their ex-husband and the children, which can lead to misunderstandings and conflicts.

2. Manipulating Custody Arrangements: They might seek to alter custody arrangements in ways that could disadvantage the ex-husband, such as requesting sole custody or limiting visitation.

3. Financial Maneuvering: Some may attempt to secure financial advantages through alimony, child support, or by misrepresenting financial situations in court.

4. Using the Legal System: They might file frequent legal motions or claims, which can be financially draining for the ex-husband.

5. Negative Influence on Children: There may be attempts to influence children's perceptions of their father, which can strain their relationship.

6. Public Defamation: Some might speak negatively about their ex-husband to friends, family, or in public, damaging his reputation.

7. Exaggerating Issues: They might exaggerate or fabricate issues regarding the ex-husband's behavior or parenting capabilities

to gain leverage in custody or financial matters. It's essential to emphasize that these behaviors can contribute to a toxic environment for everyone involved, especially the children. Healthy co-parenting involves cooperation, communication, and mutual respect. If you or someone you know is navigating a challenging divorce, seeking support from professionals, such as counselors or legal advisors, can be beneficial.

This is why you need to be prepared to have a fulfilling and happy life with the "love" of your life but also be prepared and protected against the devastating effects of a horrible divorce.

Overall, "decapitate Medusa" conveys themes of bravery, strategy, and the triumph of good over evil.

Applying this concept to marriage and divorce could be very controversial.

# THE PATH AHEAD

Divorce can feel like an overwhelming process, but it's also a chance for growth, self-discovery, and a new beginning. By understanding the emotional and practical aspects of divorce, you can approach this life transition with strength and resilience.

It's okay to grieve the end of your marriage, but don't lose sight of the opportunities ahead. With the right mindset and support system, you can navigate this chapter of your life with grace and emerge stronger than before.

> "Does speed dating necessarily end up in a quickie divorce...?"
>
> — Josh Stern

> "Divorce is the one human tragedy that reduces everything to cash."
>
> — Rita Mae Brown

# CHAPTER 2

## Things to Consider and Discuss Before Getting Married

> "Divorce is the one human tragedy that reduces everything to cash."
>
> — Rita Mae Brown

Before embarking on the journey of marriage, it's essential to take a step back and have honest, meaningful conversations about the foundation of your future together. Marriage is more than love and attraction—it's about building a life with someone whose values, goals, and habits align with your own. While no one can predict every challenge, discussing these key topics upfront can help you both navigate the complexities of marriage with greater clarity and understanding. Here are some crucial aspects to consider and address before saying "I do":

- **Religion**: Talk about your religious beliefs and practices. Do they align? If not, how will you handle differences in faith, especially when raising children?

- **Conflict Resolution, Communication**: How do you both handle disagreements? Discuss how to communicate effectively, resolve arguments, and make decisions as a team.

- **Love Language**: Learn how you each express and receive love. Knowing your partner's love language (e.g., words of affirmation, acts of service) can strengthen your bond.

- **Managing Finances, Financial Stability, Dealing with Money Stress**: Be open about income, debts, and financial goals. How will you budget, save, and deal with financial stress together?
- **Spending Habits, Financial Compatibility**: Are you a saver or a spender? Understand each other's financial habits to avoid conflicts in the future.
- **Sex**: Frequency, quality, kinky, body count; they all count! History of pedophilia, sex with animals, pornography, sexual services, Only Fans are also important points to be mindful of.
- **Dating Experience, Previous Relationships, and Prostitution**: Be honest about past relationships and experiences. Transparency builds trust and helps avoid surprises later.
- **Marriage License, No Need for One, Defining Marriage**: Discuss what marriage means to you. Ensure all legal requirements are met, and confirm no one is already married or hiding past failed marriages.
- **Shared Goals: House, Travel, Saving**: What are your shared dreams? Do you want a house, travel, or prioritize savings? Align your visions for the future.
- **Division of Household Chores**: Decide how you'll share responsibilities around the house to ensure balance and prevent resentment.
- **Kids: Yes, No, How Many, When**: Be clear about whether you want children, how many, and the timing. This can be a deal breaker if you're not aligned.
- **Career Decisions**: Discuss your career ambitions. How will you support each other's goals, and will either of you compromise for the other?
- **History of Addictions, Homelessness**: Be upfront about past struggles with addictions or homelessness.

Knowing these helps build understanding and support.
- **Discuss In-Laws: Married, Divorced, Amicable, Family History**: Talk about your families. What's their history, and how involved will they be in your marriage?
- **Estate Planning**: Plan for the future, including wills and managing shared assets, to avoid complications later.
- **Find Someone You Like a Lot Sexually, Physically, Emotionally**: Compatibility in all these areas is crucial. Ensure you're deeply attracted and connected on every level.
- **History on Social Media, Exposed Body, Comments, Likes, Bikini Pictures, Sites**: Talk about comfort levels with each other's online presence and boundaries regarding social media behavior.
- **Family Background: Comes from Money, Hardworking, Scammers, Thieves**: Understand your partner's family dynamics, values, and history to prepare for potential challenges.
- **Family Inheritance, Education, Money**: Clarify expectations around family money, inheritance, and financial support.
- **Medical History, Inherited Traits or Diseases**: Learn about your partner's medical background to prepare for any future health-related concerns.
- **Values, Morals, Integrity**: Align on core values and moral standards. A shared sense of integrity strengthens the foundation of your relationship.
- **Political Views**: Political beliefs can impact how you approach social issues, so discuss these to avoid future conflicts.
- **Vaccination Status**: In today's world, this might be an important conversation, especially regarding health choices for future children.

- **Don't Marry Potential, Marry Intelligence, Beauty, and Money**: While marrying for potential is risky, ensure your partner has qualities you value deeply—intelligence, attraction, and stability all matter.

"Divorce is success. Failure is staying married to a person you no longer love."

— Ben Tolosa,
*Masterplan Your Success: Deadline Your Dreams*

# CHAPTER 3

## Preparing for Divorce

> "I married Miss Right. I just didn't know her first name was always."
>
> — Red Skelton

Marriage is a journey filled with twists and turns, highs and lows. Prepare for the unexpected, cherish the good moments, and face challenges together with love and understanding.

If the day comes when the path of marriage leads to a fork in the road, and divorce becomes the only option, take solace in the knowledge that endings are also beginnings. Embrace this new chapter with courage, learn from the past, and open your heart to the possibilities that lie ahead.

Life after divorce may seem daunting at first, but it is also a time for self-discovery, growth, and new beginnings. Embrace the freedom to rediscover yourself, pursue your passions, and forge a path that is true to your heart.

Remember, whether you are walking down the aisle, navigating the complexities of divorce, or starting anew, the most important thing is to stay true to yourself, be kind to others, and embrace each moment with grace and resilience. May your journey be filled with love, growth, and the courage to embrace whatever comes your way.

- Acknowledge it, accept it, embrace it.
- Create space for your emotions

- Create co-parenting plan
- Value your spouse, respect your ex-partner
- Time with kids needs to be enriching.
- Engage in new activities
- Make new friends
- Rekindle your love for yourself
- If need be talk to a therapist

# PRENUP MISCONCEPTIONS

Prenuptial agreements often come with misconceptions that can lead to misunderstandings about their purpose and benefits.

Here are some common misconceptions:

1. Only for the Wealthy: Many believe that prenuptial agreements are only for the rich. In reality, anyone can benefit from a prenup, regardless of wealth, especially if there are significant assets, debts, or children from previous relationships involved.

2. They Indicate a Lack of Trust: Some think that requesting a prenup suggests a lack of trust in the relationship. However, it can actually promote open communication about finances and expectations, fostering trust.

3. They Are Unenforceable: There is a belief that prenups are not legally binding. While they can be challenged in court under certain circumstances, properly drafted and executed agreements are enforceable in most jurisdictions.

4. They Can Cover Anything: Some people assume that prenups can include any terms, like personal behavior or lifestyle choices. However, they are typically limited to financial matters and property rights.

5. They Are Set in Stone: Another misconception is that prenups cannot be modified. In truth, couples can revise or revoke their agreement at any time, as long as both parties agree.

6. They Only Protect One Party: While they can protect one spouse, prenups can also be structured to provide fair terms

for both parties, ensuring that both interests are considered. Understanding these misconceptions can help couples approach prenuptial agreements more openly and constructively.

"What did your husband do to make you leave him? He breathed."

— Pamela Hamilton,
Lady Be Good: The Life and Times of Dorothy Hale

— Helen Rowland

When two people decide to get a divorce, it isn't a sign that they 'don't understand' one another, but a sign that they have, at last, begun to.

# CHAPTER 4

## Experiencing Divorce

"Half of all marriages end in divorce- and then there are the really unhappy ones."

— Joan Rivers

Experiencing a divorce can be a challenging and emotionally taxing process. While it's natural to feel a range of emotions during this time, there are some strategies that can help you cope and minimize the negative impact of a divorce on your well-being. Here are some tricks to help you not get affected by a divorce:

1. Seek support: Surround yourself with supportive friends, family members, or a therapist who can offer emotional support and guidance during this difficult time.

2. Take care of yourself: Prioritize self-care by maintaining a healthy lifestyle, getting enough rest, eating well, and engaging in activities that bring you joy and relaxation.

3. Focus on the future: While it's important to acknowledge your emotions and grieve the loss of the relationship, try to shift your focus towards creating a positive vision for your future and setting new goals for yourself.

4. Practice mindfulness: Engage in mindfulness practices such as meditation, deep breathing, or yoga to help

you stay grounded in the present moment and manage stress and anxiety.

5. Establish boundaries: Set clear boundaries with your ex-partner to help you navigate the divorce process and protect your emotional well-being.
6. Seek legal guidance: Consult with a trusted attorney to understand your rights, legal options, and responsibilities during the divorce proceedings.
7. Stay positive: Cultivate a positive mindset by focusing on gratitude, practicing optimism, and surrounding yourself with positivity.
8. Engage in new activities: Explore new hobbies, interests, or activities that can distract you from negative thoughts and help you discover new aspects of yourself.
9. Give yourself time to heal: Healing from a divorce takes time, so be patient with yourself and allow yourself to experience and process your emotions at your own pace.
10. Consider therapy: Individual or group therapy can provide a safe space to explore your feelings, gain insights, and develop coping strategies to navigate the challenges of divorce.

Most people go through multiple phases.

1. Denial
2. Anger
3. Bargaining
4. Depression
5. Acceptance

You might be going through one of these phases, but don't worry, you will get through it like everyone else. Remember that everyone copes with divorce differently, and it's okay to seek professional help if you're struggling to cope with the emotional impact of a divorce. Taking care of you and seeking support are essential steps towards healing and moving forward after a divorce.

# COMMON COMMENTS WOMEN MIGHT EXPRESS

Common comments women might express when going through a divorce often reflect a mix of emotions and realizations. Here are some typical sentiments:

1. Relief: "I finally feel free to be myself."
2. Sadness: "I never thought it would end this way."
3. Empowerment: "I've learned so much about myself through this process."
4. Regret: "I wish I had made different choices earlier."
5. Concerns about the future: "I'm worried about starting over."
6. Support: "I appreciate my friends and family now more than ever."
7. Clarity: "I realize now what I truly want in a relationship."
8. Vengeance: "He will pay for this."
9. Guilt tripping: "Look what he did to our family."
10. Realization: "I realized I was never in love."
11. I don't need him.
12. All I need is his money.

13. I loved him like a friend.
14. He will never find someone like me.
15. Useless sperm donor
16. Baby daddy
17. He was a good provider.
18. I will find someone better.
19. I will take him to the cleaners.
20. He will never see the kids again.
21. He deserves a whore.
22. I will never get married again.

These comments reflect the complexity of emotions involved in divorce, including relief, grief, and hope for the future.

Even though you think you are getting married for life, let me enlighten you: chances are that you won't.

65% of marriages end in divorce, and the reason does not matter; women initiate the divorce 80% of the times. You are one valid excuse away from losing half of everything you built.

In the end, nothing matters; only a few things will be taken into consideration: parental agreement, matrimonial home, and division of assets.

Nothing else matters, what you did for her family and friends, how much you helped anyone cause of her; those same people will turn their back on you and will choose her side and will ghost you or ignore calls or texts.

# GATHERING FINANCIAL AND LEGAL DOCUMENTS

Sadly, the law only looks at assets and financial statements; the court system is designed to favor the partner who makes less money. So, one of the things to do to be on top of the game is to cut as much financial help from the beginning, make sure to leave only the necessary funds to survive, eventually and when the divorce is final, she or he will keep what's his or hers in the eyes of the law. Before a settlement, there is no reason for the partner who makes more to keep the lifestyle he or she can't afford. Don't feel bad or guilty about the decision; they will be okay without all the luxury you provided before. If you are the one who makes the most money and the difference in income is huge, something else you could do is to put everything in his or her name. That way, if you walk out of the relationship, she or he will be responsible for all the bills and responsibilities, while you still have the right to half of the profits when the sale of assets happens.

If you own a company, make sure to pay your partner more than you pay yourself. This way, in the event of a divorce, your spouse will end up paying you alimony and child support. This is not financial or accounting advice.

Here are some simple steps that can help make the process a little easier:

- **Organize Financial Records**: Gather all financial documents, including pay stubs, bills, and any legal contracts. Being organized can make the divorce process smoother and more transparent.

- **Bank Statements**: Collect all bank statements from joint and individual accounts to get a clear picture of your financial standing and any discrepancies.
- **Investment Accounts**: Make a list of all investments, such as stocks, bonds, or mutual funds, to ensure nothing is overlooked in the division of assets.
- **Loan Applications**: Keep copies of any loan agreements or applications, as these can provide insights into shared liabilities.
- **RRSPs**: Ensure all registered retirement savings plans are accounted for, as these may be divided during the settlement.
- **Tax Refunds of the Last 3 Years**: Gather your tax returns and refunds from the past three years. These documents are crucial for understanding income and potential claims.
- **Property Tax Bills**: Keep property tax bills handy to document real estate ownership and the associated costs.
- **Credit Reports**: Obtain credit reports for both you and your partner to identify any shared debts or financial obligations.
- **Mortgage Statements**: Review all mortgage statements to determine equity in shared properties and ongoing financial responsibilities.
- **Return to Individual Credit History**: Begin separating your financial identity by returning to individual credit accounts and building your own credit history.

- **Close Joint Accounts**: Safeguard your finances by closing any joint bank or credit accounts to avoid future misuse or disputes.

- **Understand Divorce Options**: Research and understand your divorce options, whether it's mediation, collaborative divorce, or litigation, to choose the best approach for your situation.

- **Set Goals for Mediation**: If mediation is an option, set clear goals for what you hope to achieve, focusing on fairness and long-term stability.

- **Put the Kids First**: Prioritize the emotional and physical well-being of your children. Shield them from conflict and make decisions with their best interests in mind.

- **Seek Emotional Support from the Right People**: Surround yourself with trusted friends, family, or professionals who can provide emotional stability without fueling negativity.

- **Record Everything**: Keep detailed records of important conversations, agreements, or financial transactions. This can serve as evidence if disputes arise.

- **Find Common Grounds**: Try to identify areas where you and your partner can agree to make the process less contentious and more collaborative.

- **Hire a Good Lawyer**: Invest in a competent and experienced divorce lawyer who understands your needs and will advocate for your best interests.

# BAD LAWYERS

Unscrupulous lawyers can employ various tactics to turn spouses against each other during divorce proceedings, exacerbating conflicts and creating animosity. Here are some common methods:

1. Manipulative Communication- Misrepresentation of Facts: Lawyers may distort information or present misleading narratives to provoke anger or distrust. - Selective Disclosure: Sharing only certain details can create a biased view of the other spouse.

2. Exaggerating Issues- Inflating Concerns: Lawyers might exaggerate issues, such as financial irresponsibility or parenting capabilities, to instigate fear and resentment.

3. Instigating Rivalry- Encouraging Competitiveness: Promoting a "win at all costs" mentality can lead to a focus on defeating the other spouse rather than resolving issues amicably.

4. Exploiting Vulnerabilities - Targeting Weaknesses: Unscrupulous lawyers may exploit emotional or psychological vulnerabilities, encouraging spouses to act against their better judgment.

5. Creating False Alliances- Fostering Loyalty: By portraying themselves as the spouse's only ally, lawyers can create a divide, making each partner feel isolated from the other.

6. Fueling Paranoia- Suggesting Infidelity or Dishonesty: Implying that the other spouse is being unfaithful or

dishonest can create distrust and animosity.

7. Encouraging Hostile Legal Tactics- Aggressive Litigation: Promoting a combative approach rather than mediation can escalate tensions and lead to a breakdown in communication.

8. Involving Third Parties -Using Family or Friends: Lawyers might encourage clients to turn friends or family against the other spouse, making the conflict more personal and widespread.

9. Manipulating Emotions - Playing on Grievances: Encouraging clients to dwell on past grievances can foster resentment and make reconciliation more difficult.

10. Delaying Proceedings -Stalling for Strategy: Prolonging the legal process can increase stress and conflict, making it easier for animosity to grow.

Conclusion While not all lawyers engage in these unethical practices, those who do can significantly worsen the emotional toll of divorce. It's essential for individuals to choose legal representation carefully and maintain open communication to counteract these tactics. Seeking mediation or collaborative divorce options may help mitigate conflict and promote a more amicable resolution.

**In divorce law, freezing assets refers to a legal action that prevents one spouse from selling, transferring, or otherwise disposing of marital assets during the divorce proceedings.**

This is often requested to protect the financial interests of both parties and ensure an equitable division of assets.

Key Points on Freezing Assets in Divorce:

1. Purpose: The main goal is to maintain the status quo of marital assets until the court can determine how they should be divided.

2. Legal Process: A party typically must file a motion with the court, demonstrating why freezing the assets is necessary. This may involve showing the possibility of asset dissipation or concealment.

3. Types of Assets: The assets that can be frozen might include bank accounts, real estate, investments, and personal property.

4. Court Orders: If the court grants the motion, it will issue an order directing that certain assets be frozen. This may also include restrictions on selling or transferring these assets without court approval.

5. Consequences of Non-Compliance: Failing to adhere to a freezing order can lead to serious legal penalties, including contempt of court.

6. Duration: The freezing of assets typically lasts until the divorce is finalized or until the court modifies the order.

7. Legal Representation: It is advisable for individuals involved in a divorce to seek legal counsel, as navigating asset division can be complex.

8. Jurisdiction Variations: Laws and procedures regarding asset freezing can vary by jurisdiction, so it's important to consult local laws.

Conclusion Freezing assets is a protective measure in divorce proceedings, ensuring fair treatment and preventing one spouse from undermining the financial settlement. Each case is unique, and court involvement is crucial to enforce such measures properly.

> "A divorce is like an amputation: you survive it, but there's less of you."
>
> — Margaret Atwood

# CHAPTER 5

## Dealing with the Aftermath of Divorce

"Getting divorced just because you don't love a man is almost as silly as getting married just because you do."

— Zsa Zsa Gabor

Divorce can be a challenging time for children as they navigate changes in their family structure and dynamics. Here are some important considerations and tips for parents going through a divorce with children:

# COMMUNICATION:

- Be honest and age-appropriate: Talk to your children about the divorce in a way that is honest, simple, and appropriate for their age. Reassure them that they are not at fault and that both parents still love them.

- Encourage open communication: Create a safe space for your children to express their feelings, ask questions, and share their concerns about the divorce. Listen to them without judgment and offer emotional support.

# CO-PARENTING:

- Cooperate with your ex-spouse: Strive to maintain a cooperative and respectful co-parenting relationship with your ex-spouse for the well-being of your children. Focus on what is best for the children and communicate effectively about parenting decisions.

- Consistency and routines: Establish consistent routines and rules between both households to provide stability and predictability for your children. Coordinate schedules and parenting strategies to create a sense of security.

# EMOTIONAL SUPPORT:

- Provide emotional reassurance: Offer your children emotional reassurance and support during this time of transition. Let them know that their feelings are valid and encourage them to express their emotions.

- Model healthy coping mechanisms: Demonstrate healthy ways of coping with stress and emotions to your children. Show them how to manage conflict, practice self-care, and seek support when needed.

# PROFESSIONAL SUPPORT:

- Consider therapy: If your children are struggling to cope with the divorce, consider seeking therapy or counseling for them to help them process their emotions and adjust to the changes.

- Consult with a child specialist: In some cases, consulting with a child specialist or mediator can help parents understand their children's perspectives and develop strategies to support their emotional well-being.

# FOCUS ON THE CHILDREN:

- Put your children first: Prioritize the well-being and needs of your children throughout the divorce process. Make decisions with their best interests in mind and foster a supportive and nurturing environment for them.

- Maintain a united front: Present a united front with your ex-spouse when it comes to parenting decisions and co-parenting strategies. Avoid involving your children in conflicts between parents.

# LEGAL CONSIDERATIONS:

- Create a parenting plan: Work with your ex-spouse to create a comprehensive parenting plan that outlines custody arrangements, visitation schedules, and decision-making responsibilities to provide clarity and structure for your children.

- Follow court orders: Adhere to any court orders regarding custody, visitation, child support, and other legal matters to ensure a smooth and respectful process for your children.

Divorce is a significant life event for children, and how parents handle the situation can greatly impact their emotional well-being and adjustment. By prioritizing open communication, co-parenting effectively, providing emotional support, seeking professional help when needed, and focusing on the children's best interests, parents can help their children navigate the challenges of divorce and thrive in their new family dynamic.

# DEALING WITH TOXIC FRIENDS

Dealing with toxic friends during a divorce can add unnecessary stress to an already challenging situation. Here are some tips on how to handle toxic friends during a divorce:

**Setting Boundaries:**

- Identify toxic behavior: Recognize the signs of toxic behavior in your friends, such as constant negativity, manipulation, or lack of support during difficult times.

- Limit contact: If you have friends who are toxic or unsupportive during your divorce, consider limiting your interactions with them or taking a break from the friendship.

- Communicate your needs: If you decide to maintain the friendship, clearly communicate your boundaries and let your friend know what kind of support you need during this time.

**Seeking Support:**

- Surround yourself with positive influences: Focus on spending time with friends who are supportive, understanding, and uplifting during your divorce.

- Seek professional help: Consider seeking support from a therapist or counselor who can help you navigate the emotional challenges of divorce and toxic relationships.

- Join a support group: Connect with others who are going through a divorce or have experienced similar challenges. Support groups can provide a safe space to share experiences and receive guidance.

**Self-Care:**

- Practice self-care: Take care of yourself physically, emotionally, and mentally during this difficult time. Engage in activities that bring you joy and relaxation.

- Set boundaries: Establish clear boundaries with toxic friends to protect your well-being and prevent their behavior from negatively impacting your mental health.

- Prioritize your needs: Focus on your own well-being and prioritize self-love and self-care as you navigate the challenges of divorce and toxic friendships.

**Moving Forward:**

- Evaluate your friendships: Assess which friendships are positive and supportive in your life and consider letting go of toxic relationships that do not serve your best interests.

- Focus on healing: Allow yourself time to heal and process your emotions following the divorce. Surround yourself with people who uplift you and contribute positively to your well-being.

- Forgive and let go: If you choose to distance yourself from toxic friends, practice forgiveness and release any negative emotions associated with the friendship to move forward in a healthy way.

Remember that it's important to prioritize your well-being during this challenging time. Surround yourself with supportive and positive influences that help you navigate the complexities of divorce and promote your emotional growth and healing.

# HANDLING SOCIAL MEDIA

When it comes to social media and divorce, there are several do's and don'ts to keep in mind to protect your privacy, emotions, and legal rights during this sensitive time. Here are some tips:

**Do's:**

- Review your privacy settings: Make sure your social media accounts are set to private and that you control who can see your posts and information.

- Think before you post: Avoid posting anything that could be used against you in legal proceedings, or that may provoke conflict with your ex-spouse.

- Consider taking a break: If social media is causing you stress or exacerbating the situation, consider taking a break from it until the divorce is finalized.

- Use social media for support: Seek support from friends and family on social media if you need it, but be cautious about sharing too many details about your divorce.

- Consult with your lawyer: If you have any doubts about what you can or cannot post on social media during your divorce, consult with your lawyer to get advice specific to your situation.

**Don'ts:**

- Don't post negative comments about your ex-spouse: Avoid airing your grievances or making negative comments about your ex-spouse on social media, as it can escalate tensions and affect legal proceedings.

- Don't overshare: Be cautious about sharing too many personal details about your divorce or emotional state on social media, as this information can be used against you.
- Don't post incriminating photos or content: Avoid posting photos or content that could be used to challenge your credibility or character during the divorce process.
- Don't use social media to spy on your ex: Resist the urge to monitor your ex-spouse's social media accounts or use information obtained from social media in a confrontational manner.
- Don't make major life changes public: Avoid announcing major life changes, such as new relationships or job changes, on social media during the divorce process, as this can complicate matters.

Remember that everything you post on social media can potentially be used as evidence in your divorce proceedings, so it's important to be mindful of what you share online. It's best to err on the side of caution and discretion to protect yourself during this challenging time.

# KEY FACTORS IN SEPARATION

**In addition** to the aspects you've mentioned (matrimonial home, assets division, equalization) several other factors may be involved in a separation between two people:

- Child Custody and Visitation: Determining where the children will live and how much time they will spend with each parent.

- Debt Division: Allocation of any marital debts, including credit card debt, loans, and other financial obligations.

- Health Insurance: Arrangements regarding health insurance coverage for both spouses and any children.

- Retirement Accounts and Benefits: Division of retirement savings, pensions, and other benefits accrued during the marriage.

- Tax Issues: Considerations related to filing taxes, including potential impacts on tax returns and credits.

- Personal Property: Distribution of personal belongings, including vehicles, jewelry, and other items of value.

- Business Interests: If one or both parties own a business, decisions regarding its operation and division may be necessary.

- Relocation: Considerations about one party moving to a different location and how that affects custody and support.

- Legal Fees: Responsibility for legal costs incurred during the separation process.

- Communication and Co-Parenting Plans: Establishing how the parties will communicate about the children and cooperate in parenting.

- Emotional and Psychological Support: Addressing any counseling or support needs for both parties, especially if children are involved. Each separation is unique, and the importance of these aspects may vary based on individual circumstances. Consulting with a legal professional can provide tailored guidance.

# PROTECTING YOURSELF AFTER DIVORCE

Protecting yourself from financial damage after a divorce is essential to ensure your financial well-being and stability post-divorce. Here are some steps you can take to protect yourself financially after a divorce:

1. Understand your financial situation: Take stock of your financial assets, debts, income, expenses, and financial obligations post-divorce. Understanding your financial situation is crucial for making informed decisions about your financial future.

2. Update your financial accounts and documents: Update your bank accounts, investment accounts, retirement accounts, insurance policies, will, and any other financial documents to reflect your new post-divorce circumstances. Remove your ex-spouse as a beneficiary or joint account holder where necessary.

3. Establish your own credit: If you did not have credit in your name during your marriage, establish your own credit history post-divorce by opening a credit card or obtaining a loan in your name. Building good credit is important for your financial independence and future financial opportunities.

4. Create a budget: Develop a post-divorce budget that

outlines your income and expenses. Having a clear understanding of your financial needs and resources can help you manage your finances effectively and avoid financial strain.

5. Seek financial advice: Consult with a financial advisor or planner to help you navigate your post-divorce financial situation, set financial goals, and create a financial plan that aligns with your new circumstances.

6. Consider alimony or spousal support: If you are entitled to alimony or spousal support according to the terms of your divorce settlement, make sure to understand the terms and ensure that the payments are made as agreed upon.

7. Protect your assets: Take steps to protect your assets, such as creating a trust, updating your estate plan, and considering insurance options to safeguard your financial resources.

8. Monitor your credit: Regularly monitor your credit report to ensure that all accounts are accurate and up to date. Report any discrepancies or unauthorized activities to the credit bureaus.

9. Focus on your financial independence: Prioritize building your financial independence by saving, investing, and planning for your long-term financial goals. Consider seeking opportunities for career advancement or additional income streams.

10. Take care of yourself: Remember to prioritize your emotional well-being and self-care during this challenging time. Seek support from friends, family, or a therapist to help you navigate the emotional challenges of divorce.

By taking these steps and being proactive about your financial situation, you can protect yourself from financial damage after a divorce and work towards building a secure financial future for yourself.

# COMPLETING THE DIVORCE PROCESS

To finish a divorce process, several key steps and documents are typically required. Here's a general outline:

1. Petition for Divorce: This is the formal request to initiate the divorce. It includes details about the marriage, grounds for divorce, and what is being requested (e.g., child custody, division of assets).

2. Response: If the divorce is contested, the other spouse must file a response to the petition.

3. Financial Disclosures: Both parties need to provide information about their finances, including income, expenses, assets, and debts.

4. Settlement Agreement: If the parties reach an agreement on issues like property division, child custody, and support, a written settlement agreement must be drafted and signed.

5. Child Custody and Support Agreements: If children are involved, arrangements regarding custody and support need to be established.

6. Final Hearing: In some jurisdictions, a court hearing is required to finalize the divorce, where both parties may need to present their case.

7. Judgment of Divorce: This is the final court order that legally ends the marriage and outlines the terms

agreed upon or decided by the court.

8. Filing Fees: Payment of any required court fees is necessary.

9. Service of Process: The other spouse must be officially notified of the divorce proceedings, typically done through a process server.

10. Waiting Period: Some jurisdictions require a mandatory waiting period before the divorce can be finalized. It's important to consult with a legal professional to ensure all local laws and procedures are followed correctly.

# ASSET EQUALIZATION

Asset equalization in family law, particularly during divorce proceedings, refers to the process of fairly dividing marital assets and liabilities between spouses. The goal is to ensure that both parties receive an equitable share of the assets accumulated during the marriage, which may include property, savings, investments, and debts. Here are some key points about asset equalization:

1. Identification of Assets and Liabilities: Both parties must disclose all marital assets and debts. This includes real estate, bank accounts, retirement accounts, personal property, and any debts like mortgages or credit cards.

2. Valuation: Each asset and liability is valued to determine its worth at the time of the divorce. This may require appraisals or professional evaluations for certain items, such as real estate or businesses.

3. Equitable Distribution: Most jurisdictions follow the principle of equitable distribution, which means that assets are divided fairly but not necessarily equally. Factors that may influence this distribution include the length of the marriage, each spouse's financial situation, contributions to the marriage, and any agreements made (such as prenuptial agreements).

4. Asset Equalization Payment: In some cases, one spouse may owe the other an equalization payment to achieve a fair distribution. For example, if one spouse receives

a larger share of the assets, they may need to compensate the other spouse to balance the division.

5. Legal Framework: The specific laws and procedures governing asset equalization can vary by jurisdiction, so it's important for spouses to understand their local laws and potentially seek legal advice.

6. Negotiation and Mediation: Many couples opt to negotiate or mediate their asset division, which can lead to a more amicable resolution compared to litigation. Asset equalization aims to provide a just outcome for both parties, reflecting their contributions and circumstances during the marriage.

"Marriage is the chief cause of divorce."

— Groucho Marx

"A divorce is like an amputation: you survive it, but there's less of you."

— Margaret Atwood

# CHAPTER 6

## Everyone Benefits from a Divorce

"She cried, and the judge wiped her tears with my checkbook."
— Tommy Manville

As bad as it sounds, divorce is a business and everyone involved in it will benefit one way or the other.

# BANKS

Banks can benefit from a divorce in several ways:

1. Increased Transactions: Divorce often leads to the division of assets, which can increase the number of transactions as couples liquidate joint accounts, transfer funds, or open new individual accounts.

2. Loan Services: Divorcing individuals may require loans for new homes or to consolidate debt, leading to increased mortgage and personal loan business for banks.

3. Wealth Management: Many individuals seek financial advice during a divorce regarding asset division and investment strategies, providing banks with opportunities to offer wealth management and financial planning services.

4. Fees and Charges: Banks may collect fees for account maintenance, wire transfers, or other services needed during the financial restructuring that often accompanies a divorce.

5. New Accounts: Following a divorce, individuals often need to establish new accounts, which can lead to increased deposits and account openings for banks.

6. Credit Services: As individuals rebuild their financial lives post-divorce, they may seek credit cards or lines of credit, enhancing the bank's portfolio.

Overall, the financial upheaval of a divorce can create numerous opportunities for banks to offer products and services that cater to the changing needs of their clients.

# LAWYERS

Lawyers can benefit from a divorce in several ways:

1. Legal Fees: Divorce cases often involve significant legal fees, which can be a substantial source of income for lawyers. They charge for consultations, court appearances, document preparation, and negotiations.

2. Retainer Agreements: Many divorce lawyers require clients to pay a retainer upfront, which provides immediate financial benefit and security for the lawyer.

3. Complex Cases: Divorces that involve complex financial situations, child custody disputes, or allegations of misconduct may require more legal work, leading to higher fees.

4. Referrals: Satisfied clients may refer friends or family members going through similar situations, allowing attorneys to build their client base.

5. Specialization: Lawyers specializing in family law can enhance their reputation and attract more clients by demonstrating expertise in handling various aspects of divorce, such as asset division or custody arrangements.

6. Long-Term Relationships: Divorce can lead to ongoing legal needs, such as modifications of custody or support agreements, providing lawyers with opportunities for future work.

7. Mediation and Collaborative Services: Some lawyers offer mediation services or collaborative divorce options, creating additional revenue streams while helping clients resolve disputes amicably.

Overall, the emotional and financial complexities of divorce create a continuous need for legal assistance, benefiting lawyers in various ways.

# ACCOUNTANTS

Accountants can benefit from divorces in several ways:

1. Financial Analysis: Accountants are often needed to assess and analyze the financial situation of both parties, which can lead to fees for their services.

2. Tax Implications: Divorce can significantly impact tax situations, and accountants can provide valuable advice on tax liabilities, asset divisions, and filing statuses, generating additional income.

3. Valuation of Assets: Accountants may be hired to value businesses, real estate, or other assets, which can involve complex evaluations and substantial fees.

4. Forensic Accounting: In cases involving hidden assets or financial misconduct, forensic accountants can be engaged to investigate and provide expert testimony, leading to higher earnings

5. Ongoing Services: Post-divorce, individuals may require assistance with budgeting, financial planning, ongoing tax services, and creating long-term client relationships.

6. Settlement Negotiations: Accountants can assist in preparing financial statements and reports that support settlement negotiations, providing additional avenues for billing.

7. Work with Lawyers: Accountants often collaborate with divorce attorneys, leading to referrals and increased business opportunities.

Overall, the financial complexities of divorce present accountants with various opportunities to provide valuable services and generate income.

# GOVERNMENT

Governments can benefit from divorces in several ways:

1. Tax Revenue: Divorces can lead to changes in tax filings and potential increases in tax revenue. For example, individuals may pay capital gains taxes when assets are sold or transferred.

2. Court Fees: Divorce proceedings often involve court fees, filing fees, and other legal costs, contributing to local and state revenue.

3. Social Services: Divorces may necessitate government services related to family law, child support enforcement, and welfare programs, which can lead to funding for social services.

4. Child Support Enforcement: Governments benefit from the collection of child support payments, which can help reduce the need for public assistance programs.

5. Impact on Housing and Development: Divorces can lead to increased activity in the housing market as individuals seek new residences, which can stimulate local economies and increase property tax revenues.

6. Increased Business for Legal and Financial Services: The demand for legal, financial, and counseling services during and after a divorce can boost local economies.

7. Census and Demographic Data: Changes in marital status from divorces contribute to demographic data collected by governments, which can inform policy decisions and resource allocation.

Overall, the financial and social dynamics resulting from divorces can create various avenues for government revenue and services.

# REAL ESTATE AGENTS

Real estate agents can benefit from divorces in several ways:

1. Increased Transactions: Divorce often leads to the sale of marital homes as couples divide assets, resulting in more property listings and transactions for agents.

2. New Purchases: After a divorce, individuals may seek new homes, leading to additional sales opportunities for agents as clients look for new residences.

3. Market Insights: Agents can leverage their knowledge of the local market to help clients price properties competitively and find suitable new homes.

4. Referrals: Satisfied clients may refer friends or family members undergoing similar situations, expanding the agent's client base.

5. Networking with Lawyers and Accountants: Real estate agents often work closely with divorce attorneys and accountants, creating referral partnerships that can lead to more business.

6. Investment Opportunities: Some individuals may look to invest in real estate post-divorce, allowing agents to guide clients through buying investment properties.

7. Emotional Support: Agents who provide empathetic support during a stressful time can build strong relationships with clients, leading to repeat business and referrals. Overall, the changes in living arrangements and financial situations resulting from divorce can create numerous opportunities for real estate agents.

# FAMILY MEMBERS

Extended family members can benefit from a divorce in several ways:

1. Increased Involvement: Divorces often lead to closer relationships among the extended family as they provide emotional support and help during the transition, strengthening family bonds.

2. Childcare Opportunities: Extended family may step in to help with childcare, allowing them to spend more time with children and develop deeper connections.

3. Financial Assistance: Family members might offer financial support or resources to the divorcing individual, which can foster gratitude and strengthen family ties.

4. Inheritances and Assets: In some cases, divorce can result in a redistribution of family assets, potentially benefiting extended family members through inheritances or financial gifts.

5. New Family Dynamics: Divorces can lead to changes in family structures, creating opportunities for new relationships and connections, such as with new partners or step-siblings.

6. Social Opportunities: With the upheaval of a divorce, extended family members may find opportunities for social gatherings and events to support one another, reinforcing their community ties.

7. Support Networks: Extended family can form support networks that help each other navigate the emotional and logistical challenges of divorce, enhancing their sense of belonging and community.

Overall, while divorce can be a challenging time, it can also create opportunities for extended family members to deepen relationships and provide mutual support.

# KIDS

While divorce can be challenging for children, there are potential benefits they may experience, including:

1. Reduced Conflict: If parents had a tumultuous relationship, divorce can lead to a more peaceful home environment, reducing stress and conflict that children may have witnessed.

2. Healthier Relationships: Children may benefit from seeing their parents in healthier relationships, whether with new partners or by modeling positive co-parenting dynamics.

3. Individual Attention: Divorced parents might spend more one-on-one time with their children, fostering closer relationships and providing individualized support.

4. Stability in Routine: After a divorce, parents may establish more structured routines, which can provide children with a sense of stability and security.

5. Enhanced Communication Skills: Children may learn valuable communication and emotional skills as they navigate the changes in their family dynamics.

6. Opportunity for Growth: Experiencing a divorce can teach children resilience and adaptability, helping them develop coping mechanisms for future challenges.

7. Access to Resources: Divorced parents may seek counseling or support services that can benefit the children, providing them with additional resources for emotional support. While the emotional impact of divorce can be significant, these potential benefits highlight how children can also experience positive outcomes in certain circumstances.

# FRIENDS

Friends of individuals going through a divorce can benefit in several ways:

1. Strengthened Bonds: Friends often provide emotional support during difficult times, which can strengthen their relationships and create deeper connections.

2. Increased Time Together: Friends may spend more time with someone going through a divorce, offering companionship and distraction, which can enhance their friendship. 3. Opportunities for Social Activities: Friends may engage in more social activities to help their friend cope, leading to enjoyable experiences and shared memories.

4. Personal Growth: Observing a friend navigate a divorce can inspire friends to reflect on their own relationships or life choices, fostering personal growth and resilience.

5. New Social Circles: Friends may meet new people through their friend's divorce, expanding their social networks and potentially forming new friendships.

6. Empathy and Understanding: Supporting a friend during a challenging time can enhance a friend's empathy and understanding of relationship dynamics, benefiting their own interactions.

7. Role as a Support System: Friends may feel a sense of purpose or fulfillment in being there for someone in need, reinforcing their own self-worth and social value.

While divorce can be a difficult experience, it can also lead to positive outcomes for friends through strengthened relationships and personal growth.

> "Take this marriage thing seriously – it has to last all the way to the divorce."
>
> — Roseanne Barr

# NEW SPOUSE

A new spouse can benefit from the previous marriage of their partner in several ways:

1. Financial Stability: If the previous marriage involved financial benefits such as alimony or child support, these can contribute to the household income, providing more financial stability for the new spouse.

2. Assets and Inheritance: Any assets acquired during the previous marriage, such as property or savings, may still be in the partner's name and can be used to benefit the new marriage.

3. Experience and Growth: The partner's past experiences can lead to personal growth and maturity, which can positively influence the new relationship. They may have learned valuable lessons about communication, conflict resolution, and relationship dynamics.

4. Family Connections: The new spouse may gain relationships with stepchildren or extended family members from the previous marriage, enriching their family life.

5. Shared Parenting: If there are children from the previous marriage, the new spouse may benefit from a ready-made family structure, including the joys and responsibilities of parenting.

6. Network and Support: The previous marriage may have established a support network of friends and family that can also benefit the new spouse.

7. Legal Benefits: Depending on the legal context, the new spouse might benefit from any legal arrangements made during the previous marriage, such as joint custody agreements or health

insurance coverage. It's essential for the new spouse and their partner to communicate openly about how these factors may affect their relationship and to address any potential challenges that may arise from the previous marriage.

8. The new partner will benefit from the relationship and also from the funds accumulated from the previous marriage. This experience will provide them with a fresh perspective on money and success, shaped by the sacrifices made by the former partner.

# CHAPTER 7

*Harmful Effects of Divorce*

# SUICIDE RATES AMONG MEN FOLLOWING DIVORCE

Suicide rates among men following divorce are notably higher compared to their married counterparts, reflecting the profound emotional and psychological challenges that can arise during and after the divorce process. Research shows that divorced men are approximately 2 to 3 times more likely to die by suicide than married men. The risk is even higher among younger divorced men (ages 25-34), who face unique pressures related to identity, financial responsibilities, and social expectations.[2]

Here are some key statistics and insights regarding this issue:

1. Increased Risk: Research shows that divorced men are approximately 2 to 3 times more likely to die by suicide than married men. This heightened risk is often attributed to factors such as emotional distress, financial instability, and social isolation.

2. Age Factor: Younger divorced men (ages 25-34) may experience particularly high rates of suicidal ideation and behaviors. They may face unique pressures related to identity, financial responsibilities, and social expectations.

3. Mental Health: Men going through a divorce are at a higher risk of developing mental health issues, including depression and anxiety, which are significant risk factors for suicide. Studies suggest that about 15% of divorced individuals report suicidal thoughts at some point after their separation.[3]

4. Substance Abuse: Many divorced men may turn to alcohol or drugs as a coping mechanism, further increasing the risk of suicidal thoughts and actions. Substance use disorders are frequently linked to increased suicide risk, with addiction serving as both a symptom of and contributor to post-divorce emotional distress.[4]

Contributing Factors -Emotional Distress: The emotional fallout from divorce can lead to feelings of hopelessness, worthlessness, and despair, all of which are significant predictors of suicide. -Social Isolation: Divorce can lead to a breakdown of social networks, leaving men feeling alone and unsupported, which can exacerbate mental health issues.- Financial Strain: The financial burdens often associated with divorce (e.g., child support, alimony) can lead to significant stress, contributing to suicidal thoughts and actions. One of the most devastating consequences of divorce for men is the loss of access to their children. Many courts assume that the maternal bond is stronger, leading to a bias in custody decisions. Fathers often find themselves in a position where they lose not only their marriage but also their role as a parent. This can trigger severe depression, feelings of helplessness, and suicidal thoughts. The system's failure to acknowledge the importance of a father's role in a child's life contributes to the mental health crisis among divorced men.[5]

Prevention and Support - Mental Health Resources: Access to mental health support, including therapy and counseling, can be crucial for divorced men facing emotional distress.

-Support Groups: Engaging in support groups or community programs can help reduce feelings of isolation by providing a platform for sharing experiences and coping strategies.

-Crisis Intervention: Resources such as hotlines and counseling services can provide immediate support for individuals in crisis.

Conclusion The connection between divorce and increased suicide rates among men highlights the need for targeted mental health interventions and support systems. If you or someone you know is struggling, it's important to seek help from mental health professionals, support groups, or crisis services.

# HOMELESSNESS CAN BE A SIGNIFICANT ISSUE FOR MEN FOLLOWING A DIVORCE

Homelessness can be a significant issue for men following a divorce, influenced by various factors such as financial instability, mental health challenges, and social isolation. Here are some relevant statistics and insights regarding homeless men in the context of divorce:

Prevalence of Homelessness Among Divorced Men:

1. General Homelessness Rates: While exact statistics specifically categorizing homeless individuals by marital status are limited, it is estimated that a significant proportion of homeless men have experienced relationship breakdowns, including divorce.

2. Impact of Divorce: Research indicates that divorce can increase the risk of homelessness, particularly for men who may not have adequate financial resources or social support systems.

3. Demographics: Men make up a substantial majority of the homeless population, often estimated to be around 60-70%. While not all homeless men are divorced, a significant number may have experienced marital breakdowns that contributed to

their current situation.

Factors Contributing to Homelessness After Divorce:

Financial Strain: Divorce can lead to a significant loss of income, especially for men who may be responsible for alimony or child support. Without financial stability, housing becomes the first casualty. Reports from homeless shelters show that single men, many of whom are divorced, make up a substantial portion of the homeless population.[6]

Mental Health Issues: Many divorced men may face mental health challenges, such as depression or anxiety, which can impact their ability to secure and maintain employment and housing. Many struggle in silence, with some turning to alcohol or drugs as a coping mechanism, which only accelerates their downward spiral into homelessness.[7]

Substance Abuse: As noted previously, some men may turn to alcohol or drugs as a coping mechanism post-divorce, which can further complicate their living situations and lead to homelessness.

Social Isolation: A lack of social support can increase vulnerability to homelessness, as divorced men may lose connections with family and friends during and after the divorce process. Studies indicate that single men, particularly those who are divorced, face a significantly higher risk of becoming homeless than their married counterparts.

Data and Research Insights:

Risk Factors: Studies show that single men, including those who are divorced, are at higher risk of becoming homeless compared to their married counterparts. This can be attributed to the combination of financial instability and lack of social support.

Shelter Statistics: Reports from homeless shelters indicate that a significant percentage of clients are single men, many of whom cite relationship breakdowns as a contributing factor to their homelessness.

Support and Resources- Emergency Shelters: Many cities have emergency shelters and resources specifically aimed at helping homeless men, including those recently divorced. - Support Programs: Programs that provide mental health support, substance abuse treatment, and job training can be crucial in helping divorced men regain stability.

Legal Assistance: Access to legal resources for navigating divorce-related financial obligations can also help prevent homelessness.

Understanding the connection between divorce and homelessness is essential for developing effective interventions and support systems. If you or someone you know is facing homelessness, reaching out to local shelters and community resources can provide much-needed assistance.

## Table 1: Percentage Breakdown of Homelessness Triggers (General Data)

| Cause of Homelessness | Percentage (%) |
| --- | --- |
| Loss of Job | 35% |
| Bills Higher than Earnings | 15% |
| Evicted by Family Member | 13% |
| Abuse at Home | 11% |
| Incarcerated | 11% |
| Sick/Disabled Mental Issue | 10% |
| Change in Family Situation | 10% |
| Drug/Alcohol | 9% |

# TABLE 2: RELATIONSHIP BREAKDOWN AND HOMELESSNESS (MEN-FOCUSED DATA)

| Study/Source | Key Findings on Relationship Breakdown and Homelessness |
|---|---|
| Avalon Housing (U.S.) | Estimates relationship breakdown causes homelessness in 10% of cases. |
| Chamberlain & Guy Study | Found that family breakdown accounted for 11% of adult homelessness cases. |
| Parliament of Canada Report | Marital breakdown is a key risk factor; post-divorce poverty increases likelihood. |
| Canadian Study on Older Adults | Family breakdown is a significant cause of homelessness in people over 65. |
| UK Study (2004) | Divorce increases homelessness, particularly for those over 50. |

These tables summarize both general homelessness causes and those specifically related to relationship breakdown, particularly for men.

# ADDICTION CAN BE A SIGNIFICANT ISSUE AMONG DIVORCED MEN

Addiction can be a significant issue among divorced men, often exacerbated by the emotional and financial challenges that accompany divorce. Studies indicate that divorced men are significantly more likely to develop substance use disorders, particularly alcohol and drug dependence, as a way to numb emotional pain. The lack of a support system and the overwhelming stress of financial instability can push many down this destructive path. [8] Studies indicate that for every divorced woman who commits suicide, over nine divorced men take their own lives. The loss of family, financial burdens, and a lack of institutional support create a crisis for many men, leading them to question their very existence. Here are some insights into the prevalence and types of addictions in this population:

Common Types of Addictions:

1. Substance Abuse:

Alcohol: Many divorced men turn to alcohol as a coping mechanism for dealing with the emotional pain of divorce. Research shows that divorced men are at higher risk of excessive alcohol consumption and illicit drug use compared to their married counterparts. The lack of a structured routine, coupled with isolation, can make it easy for substance use to spiral out of control.[9]

- Drugs: Some may also resort to illicit drugs or prescription medications as a way to escape their feelings or manage stress.

2. Behavioral Addictions: Gambling: Divorce can lead to financial strain, which may result in increased gambling as a means of seeking quick financial relief or as a form of escapism. Others develop compulsive behaviors such as excessive pornography consumption, gaming, or social media addiction as a means to distract themselves from loneliness and emotional distress. The need to escape reality can lead to dangerous levels of dependency, further exacerbating financial and emotional troubles.

Internet and Gaming: Some men may develop compulsive behaviors related to online gaming or social media as a way to cope with loneliness or distract themselves from their problems.

Porn: Many men look for an escape in pornography

Contributing Factors:

Emotional Distress: The emotional fallout from divorce, including grief, anger, and feelings of inadequacy, can drive some men toward addictive behaviors.

Social Isolation: After divorce, men may experience a loss of social connections, leading to increased feelings of loneliness and, consequently, a higher likelihood of turning to substances or compulsive behaviors for comfort.

Financial Stress: The financial burdens of divorce, such as alimony, child support, or loss of income, can contribute to the development or exacerbation of addictive behaviors.

Statistics and Research - Higher Rates of Addiction: Research suggests that divorced men may have higher rates of substance abuse disorders compared to married men. The National Institute on Alcohol Abuse and Alcoholism (NIAAA) notes that men, in general, are more likely than women to engage in heavy drinking and substance abuse.

Suicide and Addiction Link: The interplay between addiction and suicidal ideation is critical, as men dealing with both issues may face compounded risks. The stress of divorce can exacerbate both addiction and suicidal thoughts.

Support and Recovery: Support Groups: Engaging in support groups such as Alcoholics Anonymous (AA) or other recovery programs can provide essential emotional support and accountability. Therapy and social reintegration programs can help divorced men find healthier coping mechanisms. Encouraging social connections and seeking professional guidance are crucial steps in breaking the cycle of addiction and rebuilding a stable life

Therapy: Professional counseling can help address underlying emotional issues and develop healthier coping mechanisms.

Social Reintegration: Encouraging social activities and connections can reduce feelings of isolation and promote healthier lifestyles. Understanding the challenges that divorced men face with addiction is essential for developing effective support systems and interventions. If you or someone you know is struggling with addiction, seeking help from professionals and support networks is crucial.

# THE RELATIONSHIP BETWEEN DIVORCE AND SUICIDE RATES

The relationship between divorce and suicide rates among men is complex and influenced by various factors, including mental health, social support, and economic stability. Research indicates that divorced men are nearly 2.5 times more likely to die by suicide than their married counterparts. In extreme cases, studies have found that for every divorced woman who commits suicide, over nine divorced men take their own lives. [10]Here are some key points regarding suicidal rates among divorced men:

Suicide Risk Factors:

1. Increased Vulnerability: Research indicates that divorced men face a higher risk of suicide compared to their married counterparts. The emotional and financial stress associated with divorce can exacerbate mental health issues.

2. Isolation: Men often have smaller social support networks than women, which can lead to feelings of loneliness and isolation after a divorce. This lack of support can increase the risk of suicidal thoughts and behaviors. Many divorced men experience financial hardship, the inability to see their children, and a loss of identity, all of which are linked to suicidal ideation. The mental health impact is severe—one study suggests that approximately 15% of divorced men report suicidal thoughts at some point after separation.

3. Substance Abuse: Post-divorce, some men may turn to

alcohol or drugs as a coping mechanism, which can further elevate their risk of suicide. Substance abuse is a common escape route, with statistics showing that men who abuse alcohol or drugs post-divorce are twice as likely to attempt suicide. The combination of depression, isolation, and substance dependency creates a dangerous cycle that many struggle to break free from.

Statistics:

Higher Rates of Suicide: Studies have shown that divorced men are at a significantly higher risk of suicide compared to married men. Some research suggests that divorced men may have suicide rates that are 2-3 times higher than those of married men.

Demographic Variations: The risk can vary based on age and socioeconomic status. Younger divorced men may experience higher rates of suicidal ideation, while older divorced men may face different challenges.

Prevention and Support -*Mental Health Services: Access to mental health support is crucial for divorced men, as therapy and counseling can provide coping strategies and emotional relief.

Social Networks: Encouraging men to maintain and build social connections can help mitigate feelings of isolation and depression. While divorce can significantly impact mental health and elevate suicide risk, it's important to approach this issue with sensitivity and awareness of the broader context, including societal pressures and individual circumstances. If you or someone you know is struggling, seeking professional help is vital.

## **Suicide rate amongst divorced men**[11]

Men are 9 times more likely to kill themselves than women after divorce, study says. Men and women of this sub, have you ever had these kind of thoughts? What can we do to prevent male suicide and help men going through divorces?

Put another way, for every divorced woman that committed suicide, over nine divorced men killed themselves.

These results dramatize the terrible consequences of being a divorced man in America, and lead to the question: why are divorced men killing themselves? Some analysts argue that the research community has ignored a plausible explanation for the excess suicide risks experienced by divorced men. As Perrault[3] and Farrell[4] observe, while social, psychological, and even personal problems facing women are readily denounced, societal institutions tend to ignore or minimize male problems as evident in suicide statistics. For instance, in many jurisdictions in the US there seems to be an implicit assumption that the bond between a woman and her children is stronger than that between a man and his children. As a consequence, in a divorce settlement, custody of children is more likely to be given to the wife. In the end, the father loses not only his marriage, but his children. The result may be anger at the court system especially in situations wherein the husband feels betrayed because it was the wife that initiated the divorce, or because the courts virtually gave away everything that was previously owned by the ex-husband or the now defunct household to the former wife. Events could spiral into resentment (toward the spouse and "the system"), bitterness, anxiety, and depression, reduced self esteem, and a sense of "life not worth living". As depression and poor mental health are known markers of suicide risk, it may well be that one of the fundamental reasons for the observed association between divorce and suicide in men is the impact of post-divorce (court sanctioned) "arrangements". Clearly this is an issue that needs further investigation

# DIVORCE CAN HAVE SIGNIFICANT EMOTIONAL, FINANCIAL, AND SOCIAL IMPACTS

Divorce can have significant emotional, financial, and social impacts on both men and women in North America. Data suggests that approximately 56% of marriages in North America end in divorce, with the average length of marriage before divorce being around 8 years. Studies indicate that 80% of divorces are initiated by women.[12] Here are some key statistics and insights regarding its effects:

Emotional Impact - Mental Health: Studies indicate that both men and women experience increased levels of depression and anxiety following a divorce. However, women often report higher levels of distress and emotional turmoil.

Loneliness: Post-divorce, both genders may experience feelings of loneliness. Women tend to maintain social networks better, while men may struggle more with isolation.

Financial Impact - Income Changes: Women typically experience a significant drop in income after divorce, often around 20-30%, while men may see less drastic changes. However, men may face financial pressures due to alimony and child support obligations.

Standard of Living: Women are more likely to experience a decline in their standard of living post-divorce, while men may find their living conditions improve due to reduced household expenses.

Social Impact - Remarriage Rates: Men are generally more likely to remarry than women. Approximately 70% of divorced men eventually remarry, compared to about 50% of divorced women.[13]

Child Custody: Mothers are more frequently awarded custody of children, which can impact their financial stability and emotional well-being. About 80% of custodial parents are women.

Health Consequences - Physical Health: Both genders can experience negative health effects, such as increased stress-related illnesses and unhealthy coping mechanisms. However, men may be more likely to engage in risky behaviors post-divorce.

Life Expectancy: Some studies suggest that divorced individuals may have a shorter life expectancy compared to married peers, particularly among men.

General Statistics - Divorce Rates: In North America, approximately 56% of marriages end in divorce, with rates varying by age, education level, and socioeconomic status.

Divorce Duration: The average length of marriage before divorce is about 8 years, with many divorces occurring in the early to mid-30s. These statistics illustrate that divorce has complex and varied effects on individuals, often influenced by gender. It's essential to consider these factors when looking at the broader implications of divorce on society. 80% of divorces are initiated by women.

> "Getting divorced just because you don't love a man is almost as silly as getting married just because you do."
>
> — Zsa Zsa Gabor

# CHAPTER 8

## Potential Financial Implications for a Wealthy Individual

> "Marriage isn't all that it's cracked up to be, let me tell you. Honestly. Marriage is probably the chief cause of divorce."
>
> — Larry Gelbart

As someone who has achieved remarkable success, I wanted to share some thoughts regarding the institution of marriage, specifically, the financial implications that come with it.

While marriage can bring joy and companionship, it's essential to consider the potential risks, particularly for those with significant assets.

The financial landscape can change drastically in the event of divorce, and it's crucial to approach this personal decision with caution.

Here are a few points to ponder:

- Asset Division: In many jurisdictions, assets acquired during marriage are subject to division. This could mean substantial financial loss if the marriage doesn't work out.

- Prenuptial Agreements: While they can provide protection, not all prenuptial agreements are foolproof. It's vital to ensure that any agreement is carefully drafted and legally sound.

- Alimony and Support: Depending on your spouse's

financial circumstances, you might be liable for alimony, which can extend for years. This could significantly affect your financial stability.

- Lifestyle Changes: Marriage often leads to shared expenses and lifestyle choices. If the relationship falters, untangling these financial commitments can be complicated and costly.

- Emotional and Financial Impact: The stress of a failed marriage can take a toll on both emotional well-being and financial health, potentially affecting business decisions and investments. While love and partnership can be fulfilling, it's wise to remain vigilant about the potential repercussions on your wealth. I encourage you to seek counsel from financial advisors and legal professionals to ensure you are fully informed of your options.

If you are one of the lucky people who has inherited properties, assets or money, never mix that money. Those assets, money or properties can't be touched by the law in case of a divorce. If you use it or put it towards a new asset, you might want to acquire in your new relationship, now that money, asset or property will be split in case of a divorce.

"Love is grand; divorce is a hundred grand."

— Shinichi Suzuki

# CHAPTER 9
## Marriage

"I was married by a judge. I should have asked for a jury."

— Groucho Marx

# IS IT WORTH IT?

Whether or not it is worth getting married is a highly personal decision that varies from individual to individual. Marriage can bring many benefits, but it also comes with its own set of challenges. Here are some factors to consider when deciding if marriage is worth it for you:

1. Emotional connection: Marriage can provide deep emotional connection, companionship, and support from a lifelong partner. If you value having a committed and intimate relationship, marriage may be worth it for you.

2. Shared goals and values: If you and your partner share similar values, goals, and visions for the future, marriage can be a way to solidify your commitment and build a life together.

3. Legal and financial benefits: Marriage offers legal protections, tax benefits, access to healthcare, and inheritance rights that can provide stability and security for you and your partner.

4. Social acceptance: Marriage is often seen as a socially recognized and accepted form of commitment, which can bring a sense of belonging and validation from family, friends, and society.

5. Personal growth: Marriage can be a journey of personal growth, self-discovery, and learning to navigate challenges and conflicts in a committed relationship.

On the other hand, there are also reasons why some individuals may choose not to get married:

1. Independence and freedom: Some people value their

independence and freedom and may prefer to maintain autonomy in their relationships without the formal commitment of marriage.

2. Relationship dynamics: Marriage can bring about changes in relationship dynamics, roles, and responsibilities that may not align with everyone's preferences or lifestyle.

3. Past experiences: Negative past experiences with marriage or relationships may influence someone's decision to avoid marriage in the future.

Ultimately, whether or not marriage is worth it for you depends on your personal values, goals, and preferences. It's important to have open and honest conversations with your partner about your expectations, concerns, and aspirations to determine if marriage is the right choice for both of you. Remember that every relationship is unique, and what works for one couple may not work for another.

# ADVANTAGES AND DISADVANTAGES OF MARRIAGE

Getting married is a significant life decision that comes with both advantages and disadvantages. Here are some common advantages and disadvantages of getting married:

**Advantages of getting married:**

1. Companionship: Marriage provides emotional support, companionship, and a partner to share life's joys and challenges with.

2. Legal benefits: Marriage offers legal protections and benefits, such as tax advantages, inheritance rights, and access to healthcare benefits.

3. Financial stability: Combining incomes can lead to greater financial stability and shared expenses, making it easier to achieve common financial goals.

4. Social support: Marriage often brings a sense of belonging and support from extended family and friends.

5. Emotional security: Being in a committed relationship can provide a sense of emotional security and stability.

**Disadvantages of getting married:**

1. Loss of independence: Marriage requires compromise and can result in a loss of some individual freedoms and independence.

2. Relationship challenges: Marriage can bring about conflicts, disagreements, and challenges that require effort and communication to resolve.

3. Financial responsibilities: Sharing finances can lead to disagreements over money management and financial responsibilities.

4. Stress: The responsibilities and expectations that come with marriage can sometimes lead to stress and pressure on the relationship.

5. Divorce: If the marriage ends in divorce, it can be emotionally and financially difficult for both parties involved.

It's important to note that the experience of marriage varies for each individual and couple, and what may be an advantage for one person could be a disadvantage for another.

> "Being divorced is like being hit by a Mack truck.
> If you live through it, you start looking very
> carefully to the right and to the left."
>
> — Jean Kerr

# CHAPTER 10

# How Divorce can Harm you Financially

*"A lawyer is never entirely comfortable with a friendly divorce, any more than a good mortician wants to finish his job and then have the patient sit up on the table."*

— Jean Kerr

Divorce can lead to various financial challenges. Here are some key factors that could potentially damage someone financially after a divorce:

1. Legal Fees: The costs of hiring attorneys and other legal fees can accumulate quickly and strain finances.

2. Asset Division: The division of assets can lead to losing valuable property, investments, or savings that could otherwise contribute to financial stability.

3. Alimony/Spousal Support: Paying alimony can significantly impact one's financial situation, especially if the amount is substantial or lasts for a long time.

4. Child Support: Obligations to pay child support can also affect finances, particularly if the amounts are high relative to income.

5. Changes in Living Expenses: After a divorce, individuals may have to manage separate households, leading to increased living expenses such as rent, utilities, and maintenance.

6. Impact on Credit Score: Divorces can affect credit scores, especially if joint debts are not managed properly, leading to

potential issues in securing loans or mortgages.

7. Loss of Health Insurance: Losing access to a spouse's health insurance can result in higher medical costs and the need to find alternative coverage.

8. Retirement Savings: Dividing retirement accounts can diminish future financial security, and some individuals may find it challenging to rebuild their savings post-divorce.

9. Emotional Stress: The emotional strain of divorce can lead to poor financial decision-making, such as impulsive spending or neglecting financial planning.

10. Difficulty in Resuming Employment: In cases where one spouse has been out of the workforce, re-entering the job market can be challenging, affecting income levels.

11. Tax Implications: Divorce can lead to unexpected tax consequences, especially related to asset transfers and changes in filing status.

12. Investment Risks: Individuals may make hasty investment decisions in an attempt to recover financially, which can lead to further losses.

Planning and seeking financial advice can help mitigate these risks and provide a clearer path forward after a divorce.

"I was married by a judge. I should have asked for a jury."

— Groucho Marx

# CHAPTER 11

## Cohabitation Agreement

A cohabitation agreement is a legal document created by two individuals who live together but are not married. It outlines the rights and responsibilities of each party regarding their relationship, property, and finances.

Here are some key elements typically included in a cohabitation agreement:

**Key Components**

- Property Ownership - Specifies how property acquired before and during the relationship will be owned and divided. - Addresses what happens to the shared property if the relationship ends.

- Financial Responsibilities - Details how expenses (rent, utilities, groceries) will be shared. - Outlines how debts incurred during the relationship will be managed.

- Support Obligations

- Clarifies if one partner will provide financial support to the other in the event of a breakup.

- Dispute Resolution - Includes processes for resolving disagreements, such as mediation or arbitration.

- Duration and Termination - States the duration of the agreement and conditions under which it can be terminated or modified.

- Children - Addresses the rights and responsibilities

related to any children from the relationship, including custody and support.

- Estate Planning
- Discusses how assets will be distributed in the event of death, including whether one partner will inherit the other's property.

**Benefits of a Cohabitation Agreement**

- Clarity: Helps to prevent misunderstandings and conflicts regarding finances and property.
- Protection: Offers legal protection for both parties, similar to a prenuptial agreement.
- Customizable: Can be tailored to fit the specific needs and circumstances of the couple.
- Legal Recourse: If disputes arise, having a written agreement can provide a clear reference for legal proceedings.

**Considerations**

- Legal Advice: It's advisable for both parties to seek independent legal advice to ensure that the agreement is fair and enforceable.
- State Laws: Laws regarding cohabitation agreements can vary significantly by jurisdiction, so it's important to understand local laws. Creating a cohabitation agreement can provide peace of mind and a framework for managing a relationship, particularly for couples who want to protect their individual.

"I'd marry again if I found a man who had $15 million and would sign over half of it to me before the marriage and guarantee he'd be dead in a year."

— Bette Davis

# FUNNY PHRASES, SERIOUS REFLECTIONS

Here are some common phrases wives might say about their husbands that express humor, light-hearted punishments, or relationship dynamics:

1. "He's on a timeout."
2. "He needs to sleep on the couch tonight."
3. "I'll give him the silent treatment."
4. "He's in the doghouse for a week."
5. "He's in the penalty box."
6. "He's been grounded."
7. "Looks like he's cooking dinner tonight!"
8. "He's in the 'I messed up' chair."
9. "He's on the naughty list."
10. "He better makes it up with flowers!"
11. "He's doing extra chores this week."
12. "He's facing the 'consequences' of his actions."
13. "He'll be eating his dinner alone."
14. "He's in the 'no dessert' zone."
15. "He's on probation until further notice."
16. Happy wife, happy life.

Now, imagine you use the same phrases but mentioning her instead of him! would it be acceptable, would it be even funny?

We should reflect on what is being passed on to our new

generations through these comments.

Here are some phrases that reflect societal narratives often supporting a female perspective in relationships and separations:

1. "Behind every successful man is a strong woman.", we know this is not true.
2. "A happy wife is a happy life.", why not change it to " happy spouse, happy house"
3. "She's better off without him.", we know that in reality most women don't do better without their husband.
4. "Love yourself first."
5. "Empowered women empower women."
6. "Self-care is not selfish."
7. "You deserve better."
8. "Find your own happiness."
9. "Put yourself first."
10. "When one door closes, another opens."
11. "Healing starts with you."
12. "Strong women lift each other up."
13. "Letting go is a step towards self-love."
14. "Life is too short to settle."
15. "You can't pour from an empty cup."

These phrases often emphasize self-worth, empowerment, and personal growth, especially in the context of relationships and separations.

Here are a few witty phrases some men might jokingly say about their wives, often in a teasing or playful context:

1. "I told my wife she should embrace her mistakes. She gave me a hug!"
2. "I asked my wife for a little space. Now I'm sleeping on the couch!"
3. "Behind every great man is a woman rolling her eyes."
4. "My wife said she needs more 'me' time. I didn't realize that

meant the whole weekend!"

5. "I told my wife that I'd do anything for her. She said, 'Prove it by doing the dishes!'"

Remember, humor can be subjective, so it's always good to know your audience!

# FINAL THOUGHTS

"He taught me housekeeping; when I divorce I keep the house."

– ZsaZsa Gabor

As someone who has achieved remarkable success, I wanted to share some thoughts regarding the institution of marriage, specifically, the financial implications that come with it.

While marriage can bring joy and companionship, it's essential to consider the potential risks, particularly for those with significant assets.

The financial landscape can change drastically in the event of divorce, and it's crucial to approach this personal decision with caution.

Here are a few points to ponder:

- Asset Division: In many jurisdictions, assets acquired during marriage are subject to division. This could mean substantial financial loss if the marriage doesn't work out.

- Prenuptial Agreements: While they can provide protection, not all prenuptial agreements are foolproof. It's vital to ensure that any agreement is carefully drafted and legally sound.

- Alimony and Support: Depending on your spouse's financial circumstances, you might be liable for alimony, which can extend for years. This could significantly affect your financial stability.

- Lifestyle Changes: Marriage often leads to shared

expenses and lifestyle choices. If the relationship falters, untangling these financial commitments can be complicated and costly.

- Emotional and Financial Impact: The stress of a failed marriage can take a toll on both emotional well-being and financial health, potentially affecting business decisions and investments. While love and partnership can be fulfilling, it's wise to remain vigilant about the potential repercussions on your wealth. I encourage you to seek counsel from financial advisors and legal professionals to ensure you are fully informed of your options.

I wish you the best as you navigate these important decisions.

"Whenever your ex screams, "You'll never find another one like me!" the appropriate response is, "... I certainly hope not!"

— Unknown

# Percentage of Births Out of Wedlock (1964 vs. 2014)[14]

| Country | 1964 | 2014 |
|---|---|---|
| Chile | ~10% | ~70% |
| Costa Rica | ~10% | ~65% |
| Iceland | ~10% | ~65% |
| Mexico | ~10% | ~63% |
| Estonia | ~5% | ~60% |
| Bulgaria | ~5% | ~58% |
| Slovenia | ~5% | ~58% |
| France | ~6% | ~57% |
| Norway | ~7% | ~55% |
| Sweden | ~10% | ~55% |
| Belgium | ~5% | ~50% |
| Denmark | ~7% | ~50% |
| Portugal | ~5% | ~49% |
| Netherlands | ~4% | ~48% |
| United Kingdom | ~7% | ~47% |
| Hungary | ~5% | ~45% |
| New Zealand | ~5% | ~44% |
| Czech Republic | ~5% | ~43% |
| Latvia | ~5% | ~42% |
| Finland | ~5% | ~41% |

| | | |
|---|---|---|
| Spain | ~5% | ~40% |
| Austria | ~5% | ~38% |
| United States | ~6% | ~40% |
| Luxembourg | ~5% | ~37% |
| Slovak Republic | ~5% | ~35% |
| Ireland | ~3% | ~33% |
| Germany | ~5% | ~32% |
| Australia | ~5% | ~31% |
| Canada | ~5% | ~30% |
| Romania | ~5% | ~28% |
| Lithuania | ~5% | ~26% |
| Italy | ~3% | ~25% |
| Malta | ~2% | ~24% |
| Poland | ~5% | ~22% |
| Switzerland | ~5% | ~21% |
| Cyprus | ~3% | ~20% |
| Croatia | ~5% | ~18% |
| Greece | ~3% | ~12% |
| Israel | ~2% | ~10% |
| Turkey | ~2% | ~8% |
| Japan | ~2% | ~5% |
| South Korea | ~2% | ~2% |

# PERCENT OF US BIRTHS OUTSIDE OF WEDLOCK BY MAJOR GROUP (1964-2014)[15]

| Year | Black | Hispanic | Total | White |
|------|-------|----------|-------|-------|
| 1964 | ~25%  | ~10%     | ~7%   | ~5%   |
| 1980 | ~50%  | ~25%     | ~18%  | ~10%  |
| 1990 | ~62%  | ~35%     | ~28%  | ~15%  |
| 2000 | ~67%  | ~40%     | ~33%  | ~22%  |
| 2014 | ~72%  | ~53%     | ~40%  | ~30%  |

## Percent of Children Living with Two Cohabiting Parents vs. Sole Parent (2014)[16]

| Country | Two Cohabiting Parents | Sole Parent |
| --- | --- | --- |
| Estonia | 31% | 16% |
| Sweden | 26% | 17% |
| Slovenia | 25% | 14% |
| France | 25% | 22% |
| Iceland | 25% | 20% |
| Norway | 23% | 16% |
| Bulgaria | 22% | 17% |
| Finland | 19% | 14% |
| Belgium | 18% | 24% |
| Hungary | 17% | 21% |
| Czech Republic | 16% | 15% |
| Latvia | 16% | 31% |
| Canada | 15% | 21% |
| Poland | 15% | 10% |
| Netherlands | 15% | 13% |
| United Kingdom | 14% | 23% |
| Ireland | 13% | 19% |
| Portugal | 12% | 20% |
| Luxembourg | 11% | 16% |

| | | |
|---|---|---|
| **Denmark** | 10% | 23% |
| **Austria** | 10% | 21% |
| **Spain** | 8% | 16% |
| **Germany** | 8% | 16% |
| **Switzerland** | 7% | 12% |
| **Italy** | 6% | 13% |
| **Slovak Republic** | 6% | 11% |
| **Romania** | 5% | 10% |
| **United States** | 4% | 29% |
| **Cyprus** | 2% | 12% |
| **Croatia** | 2% | 10% |
| **Malta** | 2% | 20% |
| **Greece** | 1% | 8% |

---

[1] https://vocal.media/marriage/stupid-thing-a-wife-can-do-to-mess-up-her-marriage

[2] https://mensdivorce.com/suicide-rates-high-divorced-men/

[3] https://www.psychologytoday.com/us/blog/acquainted-the-night/201906/divorce-is-risk-factor-suicide-especially-men

[4] https://pmc.ncbi.nlm.nih.gov/articles/PMC5928459/

[5] https://ir.law.fsu.edu/cgi/viewcontent.cgi?article=1419&context=lr&utm

[6] https://thehomemoreproject.org/marital-and-family-issues-and-its-connection-to-homelessness/

[7] https://americanaddictioncenters.org/rehab-guide/addiction-statistics-demographics

[8] https://pmc.ncbi.nlm.nih.gov/articles/PMC5928459/

[9] htttps://pmc.ncbi.nlm.nih.gov/articles/PMC5928459/

[10] https://www.psychologytoday.com/us/blog/acquainted-the-night/201906/divorce-is-risk-factor-suicide-especially-men

[11] https://www.ncbi.nlm.nih.gov/pmc/articles/PMC1732362/pdf/v057p00993.pdf

[12] https://www.modernfamilylaw.com/resources/top-10-divorce-statistics-you-need-to-know/

[13] https://www.pewresearch.org/social-trends/2014/11/14/chapter-2-the-demographics-of-remarriage/

[14] Adapted from OECD data on births out of wedlock.

[15] US National Center for Health Statistics

[16] OECD

www.ingramcontent.com/pod-product-compliance
Lightning Source LLC
LaVergne TN
LVHW051526070426
835507LV00023B/3323